PERSPECTIVES ON EPFL

PERSPECTIVES ON EPFL

SCIENCE
Catherine Leutenegger

ARCHITECTURE
Bogdan Konopka

PEOPLE
Olivier Christinat

EPFL PRESS

To Maurice Cosandey, founding father of EPFL

9 FOREWORD
Tatyana Franck

13 SCIENCE
Catherine Leutenegger
47 ARCHITECTURE
Bogdan Konopka
81 PEOPLE
Olivier Christinat

117 EPFL IN THE WORDS OF ITS PRESIDENTS

119 EPFL CREATED BY A UNANIMOUS VOTE
Maurice Cosandey
121 BRANCHING OUT INTO NEW FIELDS
Jean-Claude Badoux
123 LONG LIVE EPFL!
Patrick Aebischer
125 EPFL — YOUNG AND PROUD
Martin Vetterli

127 EPFL — A BRIEF HISTORY

130 ACKNOWLEDGMENTS
131 IMPRESSUM

CONTENTS

EPFL owes its existence to Maurice Cosandey, who passed away just as the School was getting ready to mark its 50th anniversary. A civil engineer by training, Maurice Cosandey drove the School's transformation into a Swiss federal institute of technology on equal terms with its sister school, ETH Zurich. He was a visionary and forward thinker who managed to convince people of the benefits — which seem so obvious to us today — of bringing together a number of apparently diverse yet highly complementary fields in order to make the most of available skills and resources.

This groundbreaking approach is now widely practiced. Once EPFL had become a federal institution and was no longer financed by the Canton of Vaud, it opened outposts in Fribourg (EPFL Fribourg), Neuchâtel (Microcity) and Sion (EPFL Valais-Wallis). It also has laboratories on Campus Biotech in Geneva.

The Musée de l'Elysée and EPFL team up regularly on research projects involving the Museum's collections, as well as on other editorial and artistic ventures. This is part and parcel of the Museum's push to expand the multifaceted relationship between art and science. After all, doesn't the field of photography owe its existence and ongoing evolution to scientific progress? Our kinship with science also explains why the Musée de l'Elysée holds the world's largest collection of prisms created by Gabriel Lippmann, who won the Nobel Prize for Physics in 1908 for his work on the wave theory of light. And since the Museum — a "museum for photography" — recently celebrated its 30th anniversary, it

FOREWORD

Tatyana Franck
Director of the Musée de l'Elysée

seemed only fitting for us to be involved in EPFL's golden jubilee as well.

EPFL President Martin Vetterli decided to honor EPFL's extraordinary journey with a year full of events designed to celebrate science, research, education and innovation. He and I also came up with the idea of a book of photos that would illustrate the School's strategic priorities for the coming years, which include experiential learning, open science and digital technologies.

A BOOK OF PHOTOS, YET WITH A FOCUS ON PHOTOGRAPHERS. THREE PERSPECTIVES, THREE APPROACHES, WHICH COMBINE TO CREATE A COHERENT VISION OF EPFL'S PRESENT AND FUTURE.

A book of photos, yet with a focus on photographers — three to be precise — who were each given free rein to capture, in 30 images, what EPFL is today and where it is headed. Rather than mapping out the School's history, our aim was to highlight a moment in time through three themes — science, architecture and people — each of which already forms an integral part of the photographers' respective portfolios. Three perspectives, three approaches, which combine to create a coherent vision of EPFL's present and future.

Switzerland boasts an extraordinarily rich cultural scene, and Lausanne — with 22 museums for just 150,000 inhabitants — is no exception. The city's dynamic student population, one of the densest in Europe, has something to do with that. Each day, the EPFL campus comes alive with more than 15,000 people, including some 11,200 students and 347 professors working alongside scientific and technical staff and the entrepreneurs in EPFL Innovation Park. More than 115 nationalities are represented at the School, and 60% of students and teaching staff come from outside Switzerland.

The campus itself is home to two museums: Archizoom, which is dedicated to architecture, and the Bolo Museum, which looks at computer science. But this sort of historical perspective is obviously just one small part of the School — the science being carried out by

AT TIMES, AS PART OF HER THEAT-RICAL *MISE EN ABYME*, CATHERINE LEUTENEGGER BRINGS SCIENTIFIC EQUIPMENT INTO THE PHOTOGRAPHIC PROCESS.

EPFL's 20 institutes and more than 350 laboratories is resolutely forward-looking. And this is what photographer Catherine Leutenegger beckons us to discover. She has received several awards for her work, including the Manor Prize, the Raymond Weil International Photography Award, and Swiss Federal Design Awards in 2006 and 2008. For this book, she pulls back the curtain on EPFL's labs, revealing their choreography, props and inner workings with an amused and curious eye.

At times, as part of her theatrical *mise en abyme*, Catherine Leutenegger brings scientific equipment into the photographic process — in one instance capturing a mouse embryo with a microscope. In cryptographic images such as these, which she reproduces with only minimal intervention, she blurs the borders between created (or found) images and reappropriated ones. Some of the images involve cutting-edge techniques, like the photogram of white waves on a black background created via CT scan, or the image of a mouse's brain that shows the raw file produced by the scanner before the algorithm creates the final X-ray.

In her exploration of scientific research, Catherine Leutenegger conveys its diversity, from the infinitely large to the infinitely small, making the most of her access to the laboratories, the equipment, the professors and even some of the research in progress. Unlike in Olivier Christinat's work, which frames the bustling student life on campus, the researchers themselves are often absent from Catherine Leutenegger's images. Their presence can nevertheless be felt in both the order and disorder they generate.

Bogdan Konopka's approach is to strip EPFL's buildings down to their still life form. This photographer, who won the second Vevey International Photo Award, run by Festival Images, in 1998, seeks to capture the soul of a

THE PHOTOGRAPHS OF BOGDAN KONOPKA BREATHE LIFE INTO THE BUILDINGS THEY PORTRAY.

place and the memory of time. Although devoid of human presence, his photographs breathe life into the buildings they portray. The School's physical grounds are indeed in constant flux — over time, numerous buildings have been added to this large campus on the shores of Lake Geneva. Recent additions include the Rolex Learning Center, which was designed by Japanese architecture firm SANAA and holds EPFL's library — a public space that is home to over 500,000 documents. The SwissTech Convention Center, which opened in 2014, is another example. To vary the exposure, Bogdan Konopka uses three formats: two 4 x 5 view cameras (Japanese format) and an 8 x 10-inch view camera (US format).

Bogdan Konopka is particularly drawn to shadows, both literally and in keeping with the very nature of photography. In his work, timelessness prevails: "Even modern-day architecture is photographed as if it were 1,000 years old." His grainy urban landscapes seize your attention with magnetic force. Rather than set foot in the labs, Konopka preferred to roam the building tops and shoot from a bird's-eye view, revealing the campus's architectural workings from above.

Like the other two photographers, Olivier Christinat, winner of the Rado Star Prize Switzerland 2013, was given access to the entire campus, which he visited around 40 times. He is an old hand at capturing the anniversary celebrations of local institutions, having

AS HE OFTEN DOES, OLIVIER CHRISTINAT DISCREETLY IMMERSED HIMSELF IN EPFL LIFE.

been involved in the Musée de l'Elysée's "Un autre regard sur Paléo" exhibition to mark the 40th anniversary of the Paléo Music Festival, and the Museum's own 30th anniversary commemoration. For those projects, he was honoring the past and, above all, creating new memories through his work. This time around, as he often does, Olivier Christinat discreetly immersed himself in EPFL life. Blending in with the crowd gives him a unique perspective: "That's what fascinates me about photographing real life: something always ends up happening, and that something is never very different from what you had hoped for."

In his portraits, he zeroes in on simple and subtle gestures rather than attempting to isolate character traits or dramatize scenes. His images are a constant game of hide and seek, as the faces of the men and women interact and overlap. Chance being a wanderer's best friend, Olivier Christinat had very little reframing to do; the words of John Stuart Mill — "photography is a

brief complicity between foresight and luck" — are apt here. Some of the shots taken from above, despite the clarity of certain faces in the crowd, depict the depth of life rather than focusing narrowly on a particular subject. The photographer used a full-format camera to enhance the contrast between the blurred and the clearly defined, and a medium-format camera with a very powerful lens to provide greater depth of field. At times, Olivier Christinat's work resembles an altered view of reality, with his colliding perspectives and converging camera shots.

We are pleased to once again be partnering with EPFL, this time as it marks its 50th anniversary. In addition to reaffirming our commitment to supporting photographic production, this is also an excellent opportunity to deepen the relationship between art and science, as part of the ongoing quest to make sense of a complex and rapidly changing world.

SCIENCE

Catherine Leutenegger

Catherine Leutenegger was born in 1983 and obtained a Master's in Photography from the Lausanne University of Art and Design (ECAL) in 2007. She is a visual artist, photographer and teacher and has received several awards for her work, including the Manor Award, the Prix Culturel de la Photographie (awarded by the Fondation Vaudoise pour la Culture), and two Swiss Design Awards. Thanks in part to these distinctions, she was given her own solo exhibition at the Musée de l'Elysée, published a monograph entitled *Hors-champ*, and joined an artist residency program in New York City. During her time in the United States, she immersed herself in the city of Rochester, which is where Kodak was founded in 1881, and produced a book entitled *Kodak City* that records a watershed moment in the history of photography. Since 2014, Catherine has developed a multi-disciplinary approach to her art that plays with media, scale, space and the ambiguity of forms. Adopting the perspective of an archeologist and anthropologist, she explores the omnipresence of digital technology and the materialization of the virtual world. Her work has been exhibited and published around the world and is featured in several public and private collections, including those of the MAST Foundation, the Musée Nicéphore-Niépce, Banque Cantonale Vaudoise and the Musée de l'Elysée in Lausanne.

CATHERINE LEUTENEGGER

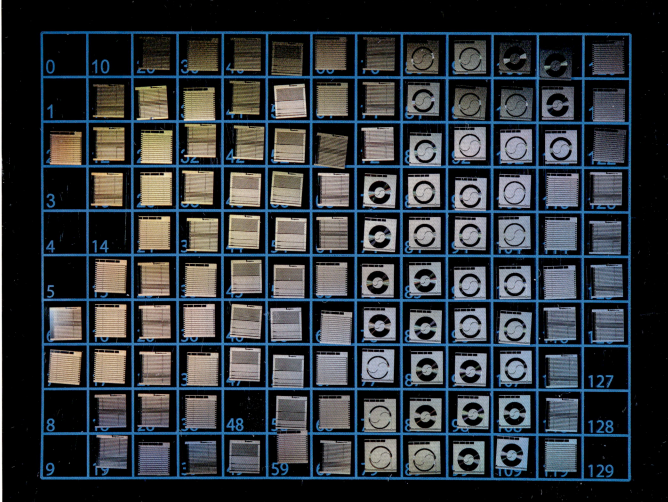

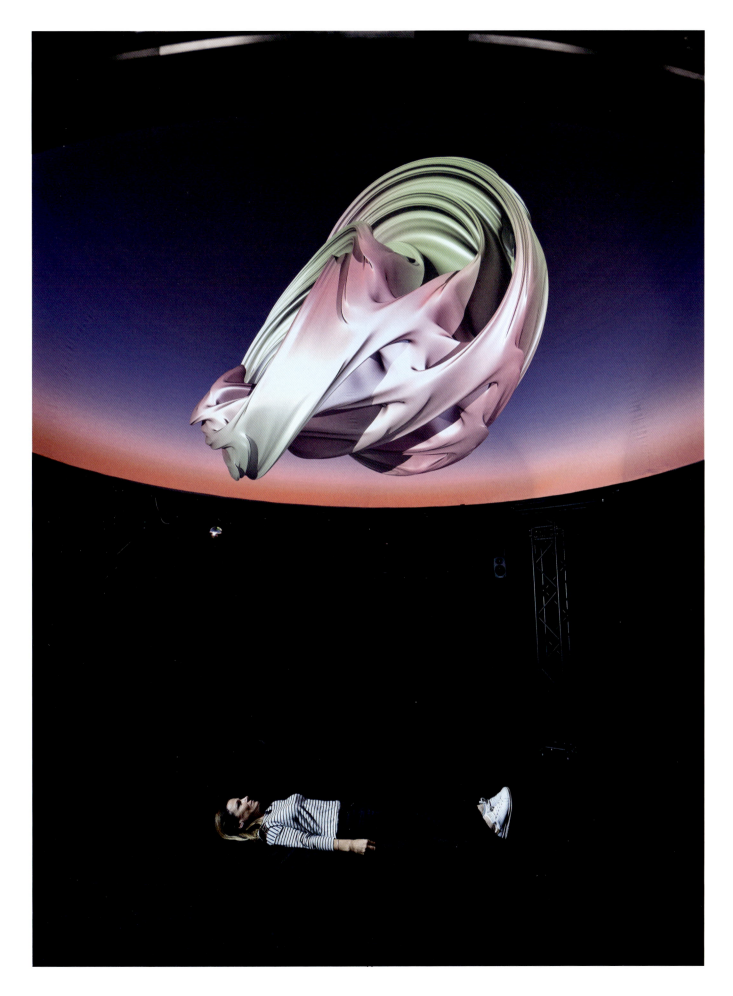

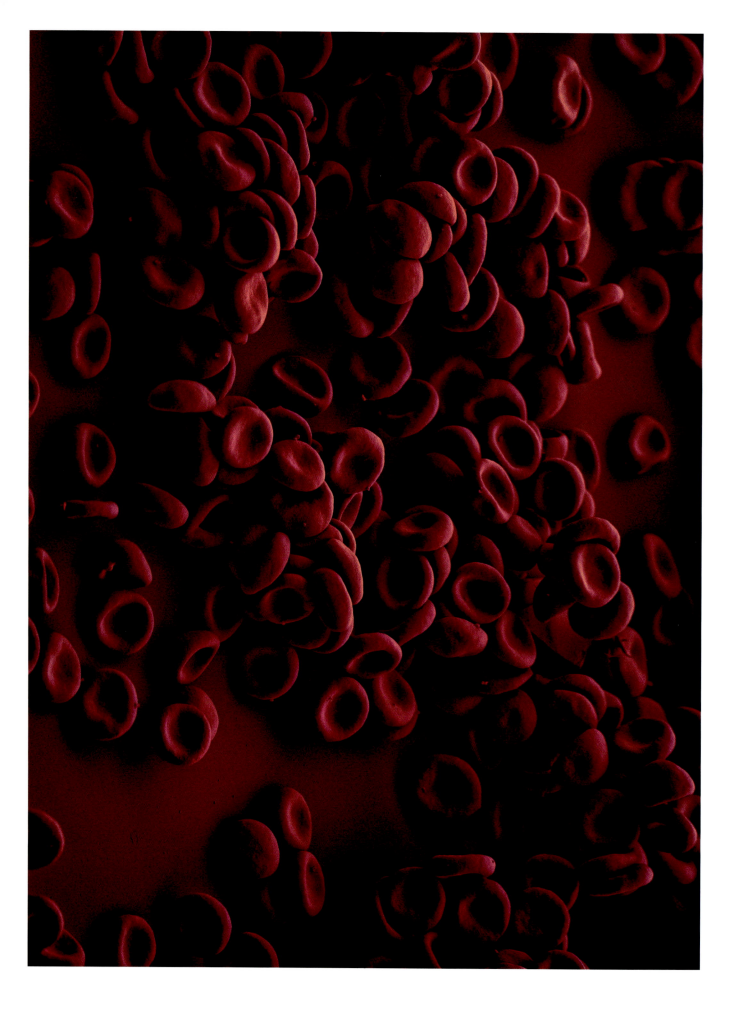

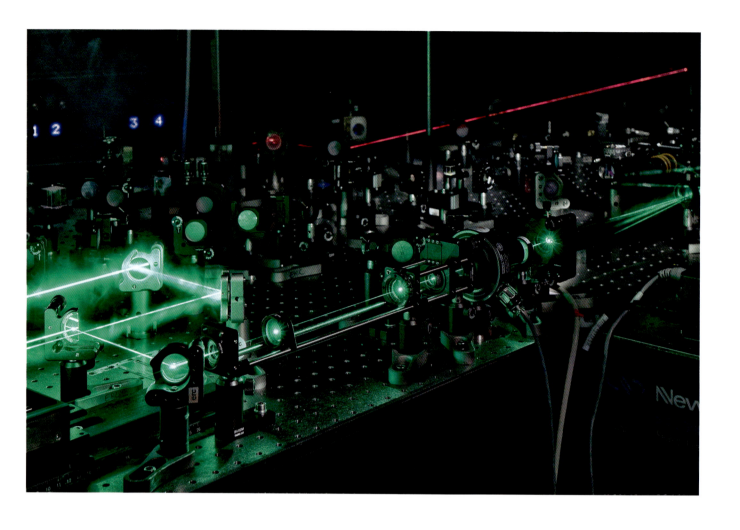

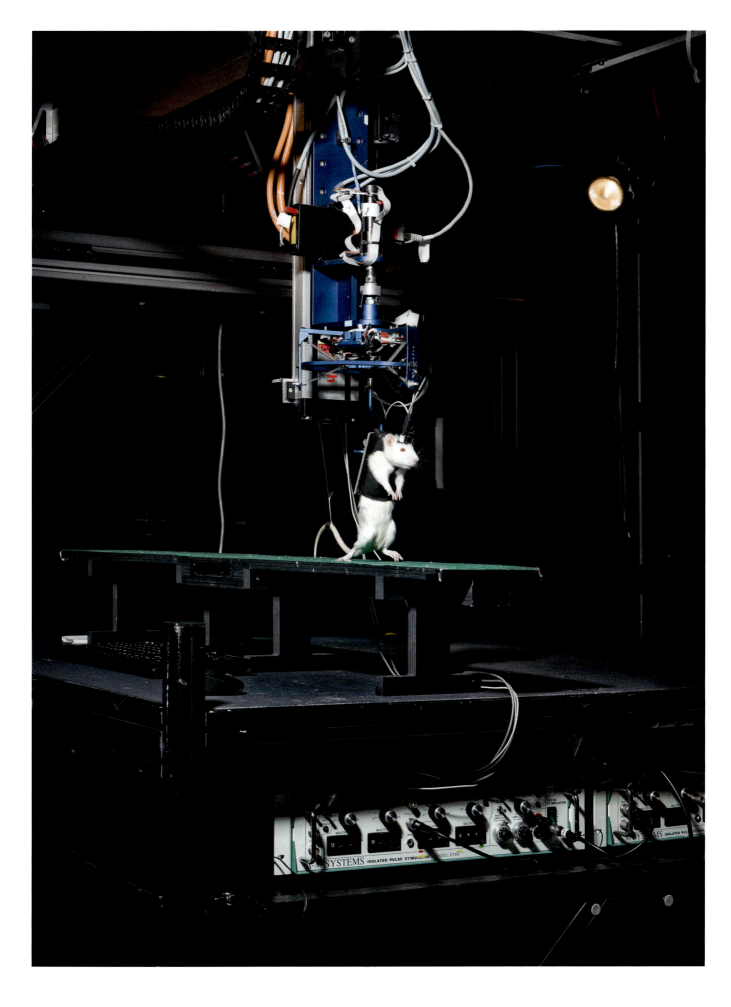

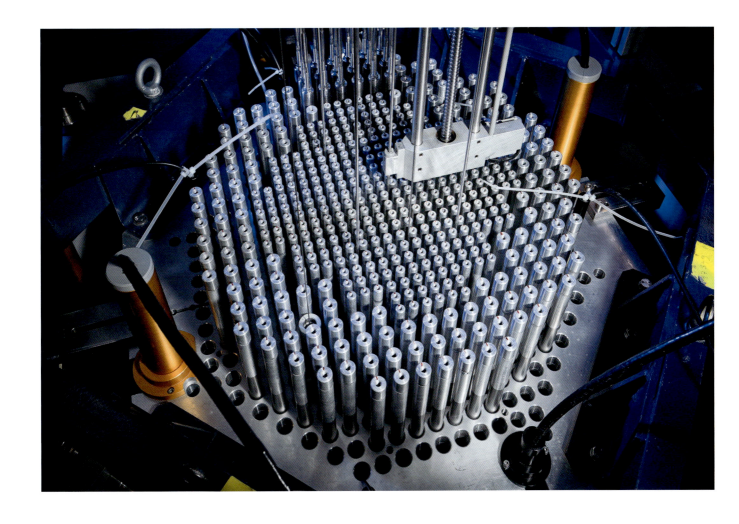

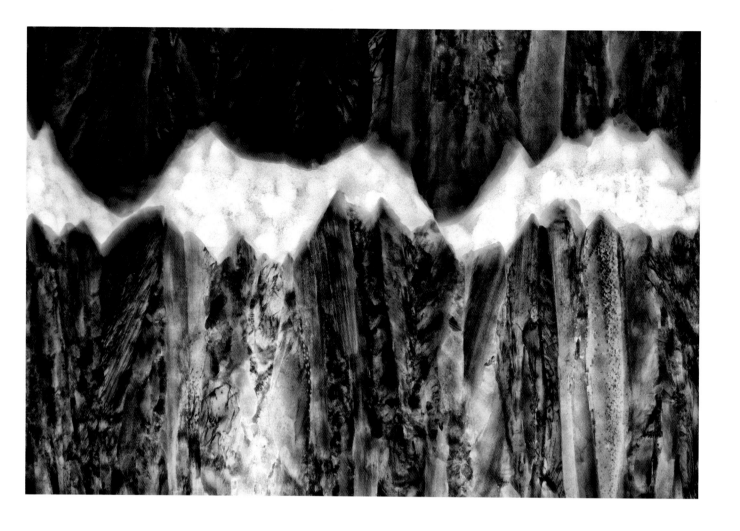

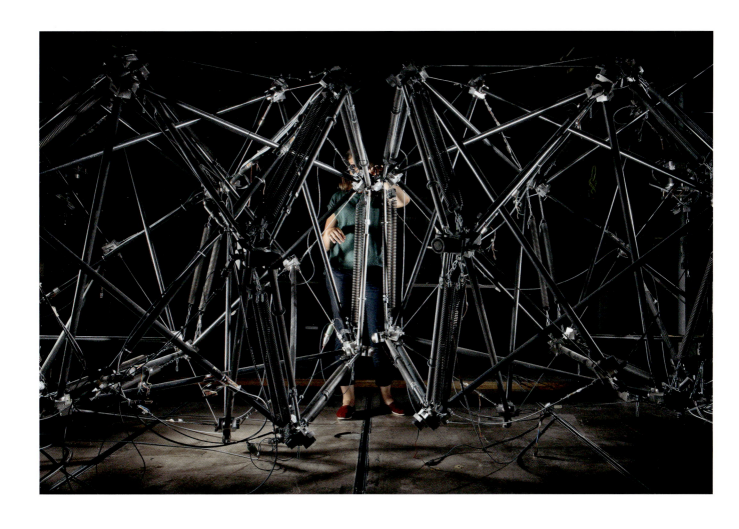

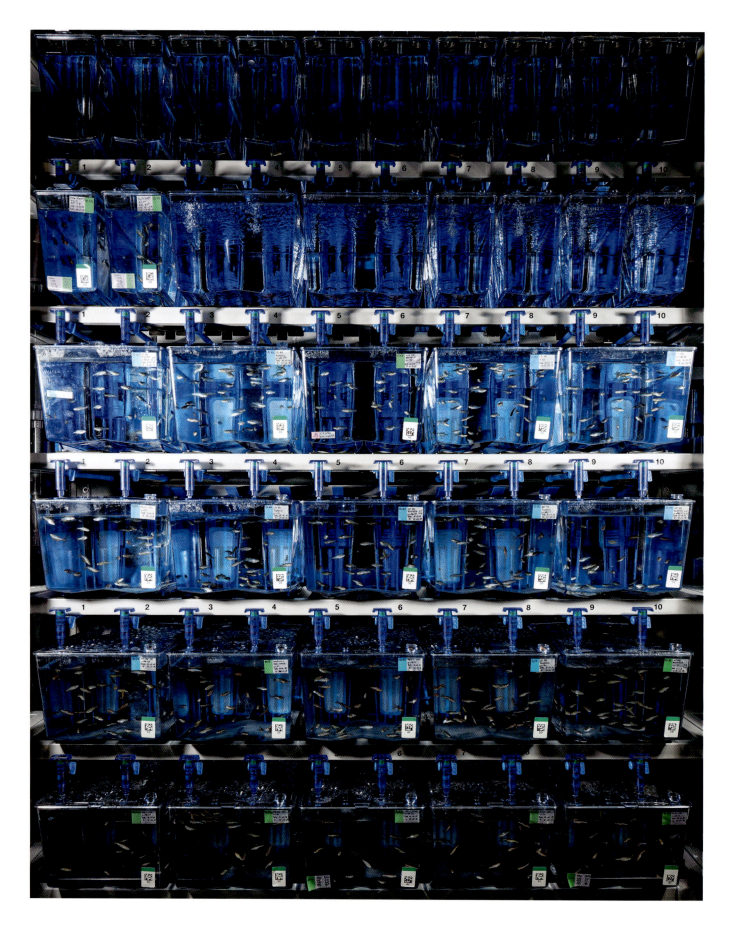

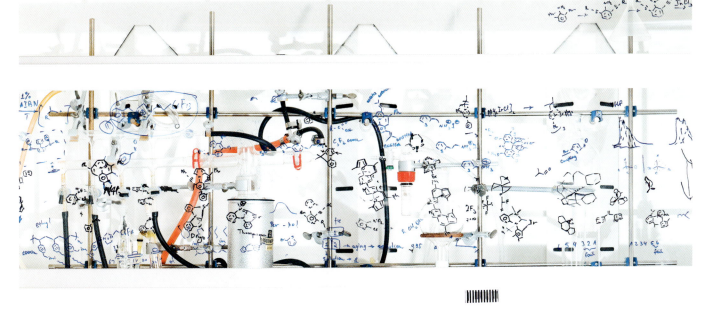

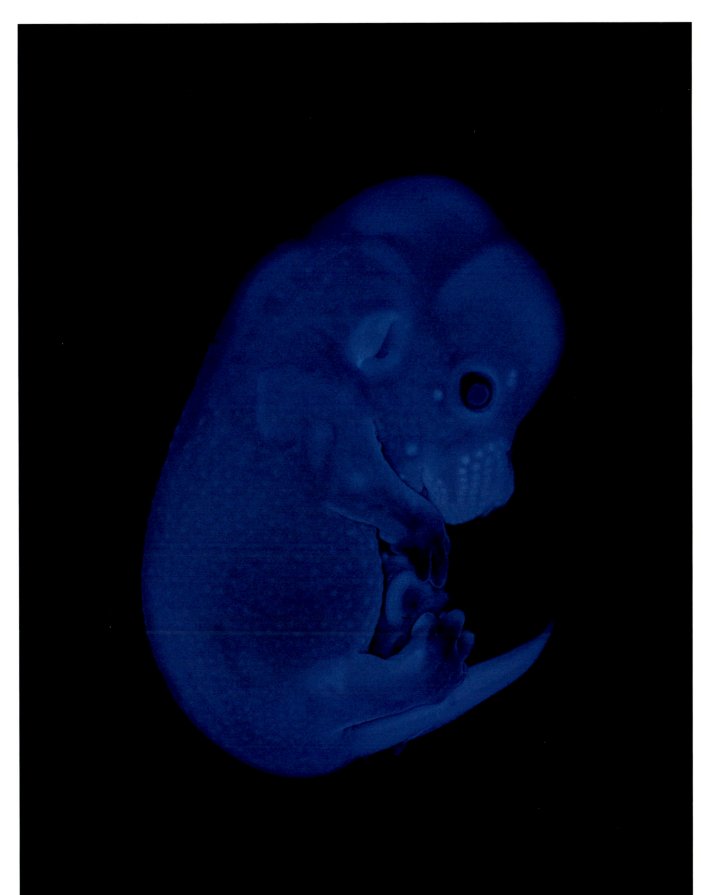

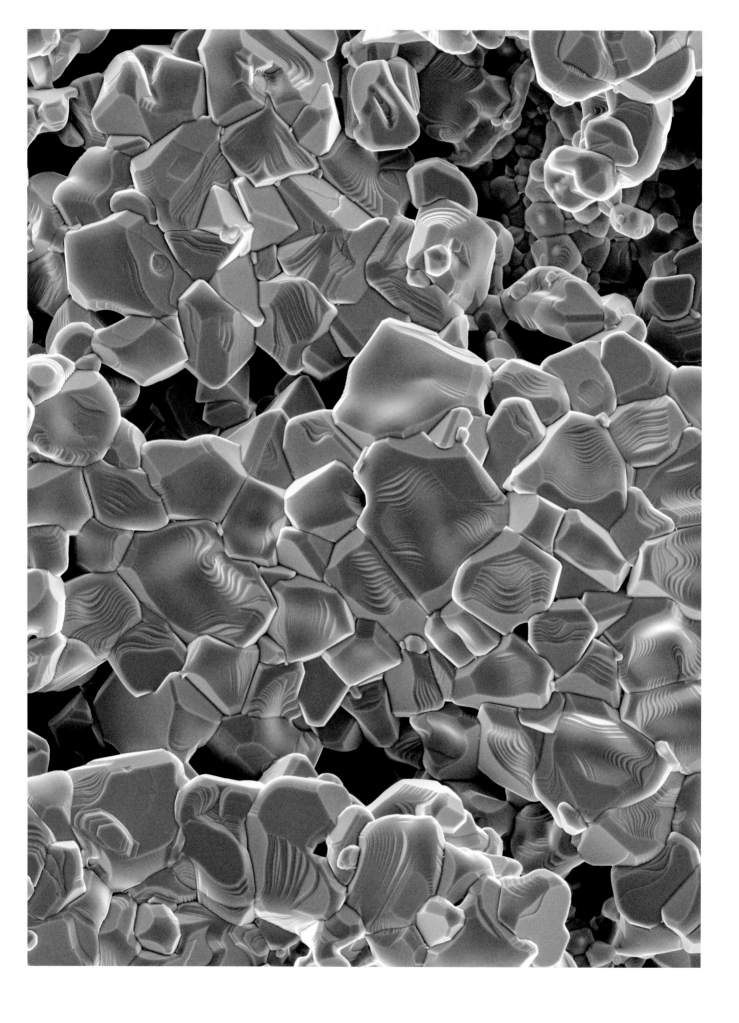

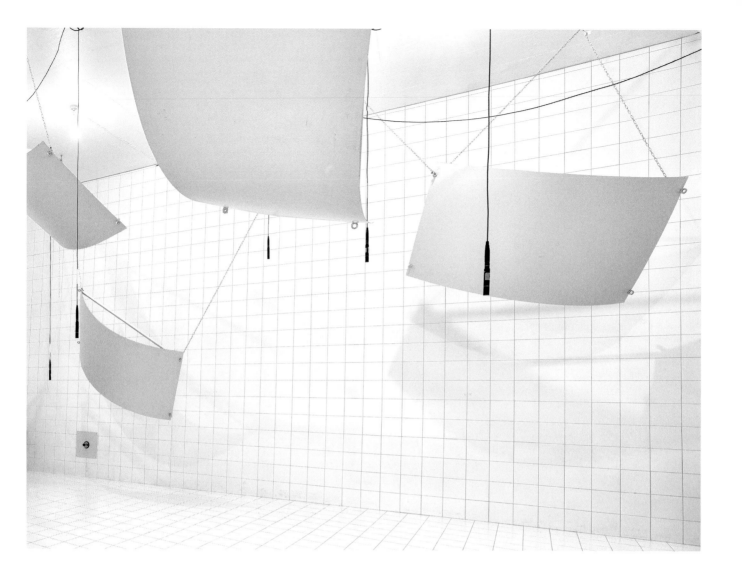

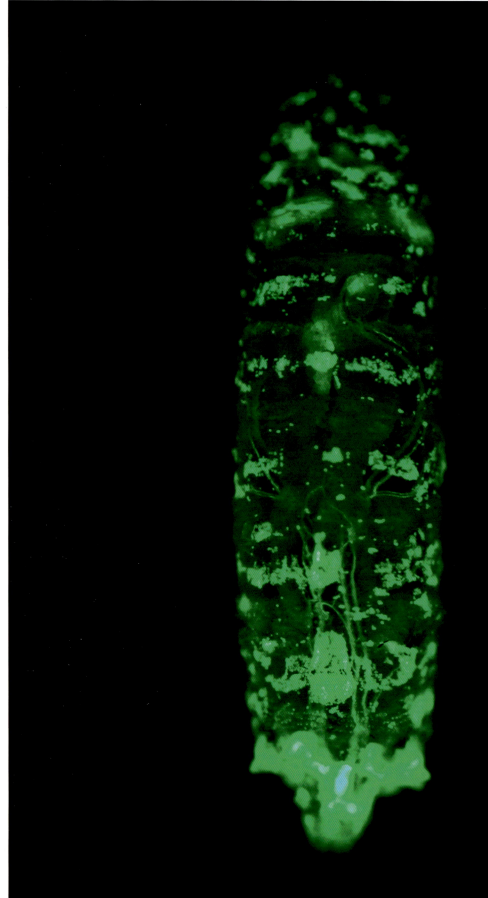

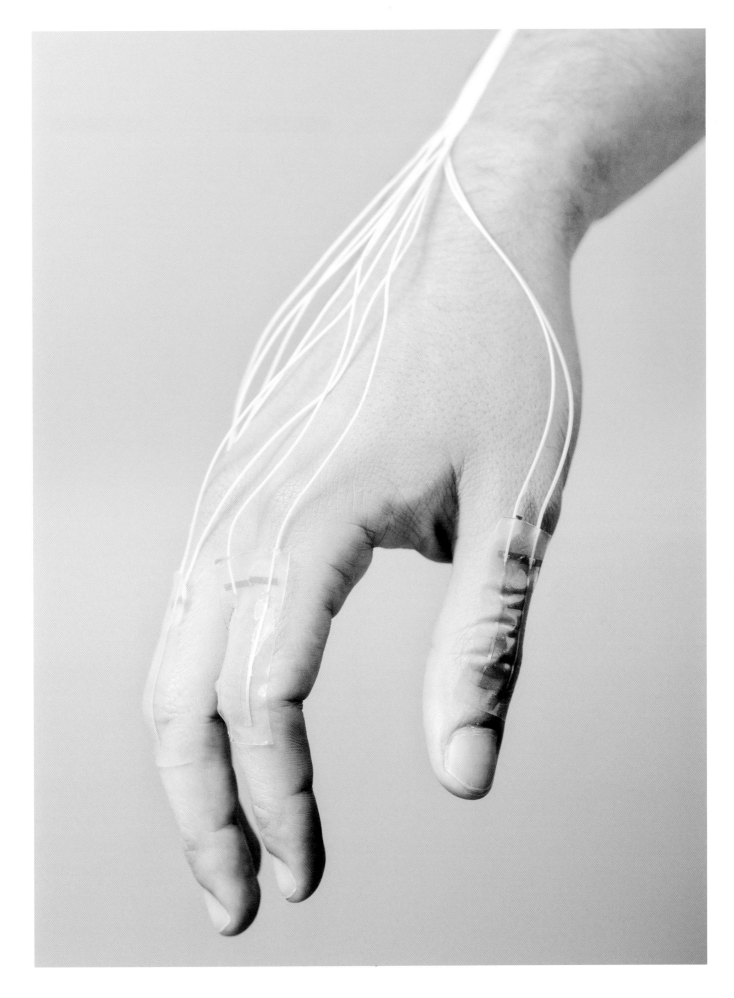

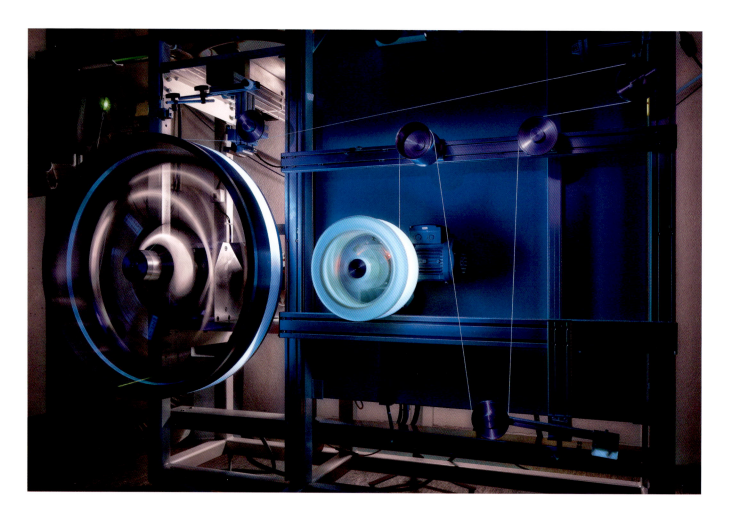

Catherine Leutenegger — Science

Photo captions

Page 15 — A true color image of chemical vapor transport crystals of Cu3(SeO3)2Cl2 produced in the Crystal Growth Facility in the Institute of Physics.

Page 16 — Photonic microchips produced in the Center of MicroNano-Technology and used by teams in Tobias Kippenberg's Laboratory of Photonics and Quantum Measurements. They contain optical 'waveguides' that direct light at the enormous intensities required to generate new frequencies of laser light.

Page 17 — Quaternion fractal visualization produced by Paul Bourke in an interactive full dome. Laboratory for Experimental Museology, Sarah Kenderdine.

Page 18 — The red blood cells of EPFL President Martin Vetterli captured by a scanning electron microscope. Each cell has a diameter of 7-8 microns. BioEM Facility, Graham Knott.

Page 19 — These sinograms combine several X-ray images from different angles to reconstruct a 3D image of an ex vivo mouse brain. This is done using X-ray computed tomography. Biomedical Imaging Group, Michaël Unser.

Page 20 — These ultrashort and intense green optical pulses generated by laser sources are used to sense tiny changes in transparent materials down to the picosecond. The aim of this research project is to develop novel material processing methods, paving the way for new types of devices with applications in optics, biotechnology and micromechanics. Galatea Laboratory, Yves Bellouard.

Page 21 — Severe spinal cord injuries can result in a range of disabilities, including permanent motor impairment. Professor Courtine's team has developed a therapy that enables fully paralyzed rats to regain supraspinal control of their leg movements. Courtine-Lab, Grégoire Courtine.

Page 22 — Carbon plate covering the interior surface of the Variable Configuration Tokamak. It protects the surface from plasma, which can reach temperatures higher than at the center of the sun. Swiss Plasma Center, Ambrogio Fasoli.

Page 23 — CROCUS is an experimental nuclear reactor used to teach and conduct research in radiation and reactor physics. Laboratory for Reactor Physics and Systems Behaviour, Andreas Pautz.

Page 24 — Transmission electron microscopy image of a thin film of nanocrystalline zinc oxide, which is used in solar cells. The film is just 4.1 microns wide. Electron Spectrometry and Microscopy Laboratory, Cécile Hébert, and Photovoltaics and Thin Film Electronics Laboratory, Christophe Ballif.

Page 25 — Tensegrity structures are mobile structures capable of changing shape and size. They can be optimized and controlled through simulations that are fed into a random search algorithm and combined with various measurements. Applied Computing and Mechanics Laboratory, Ian Smith.

Pages 26-27 — In the Cellulo project, robots replace pencils. Swarm robots, each very simple and affordable, are used on large paper sheets containing learning activities. Computer-Human Interaction in Learning and Instruction Laboratory, Pierre Dillenbourg.

Page 28 — These 18 light sources can mimic the equivalent of several thousand times the sun's radiation received on earth, with unparalleled power and precision. Laboratory of Renewable Energy Science and Engineering, Sophia Haussener.

Page 29 — Developed as part of the EU-funded ASSISIbf project, RiBot is used to study interactions between robots and fish. The robot, which is capable of influencing a school's decisions, is flexible, measures just 60 mm in length, and has a working caudal fin. Robotic Systems Laboratory, Francesco Mondada.

Page 30 — This robotic hand, named Allegro, includes Tekscan tactile sensors that can make a grasping gesture without visual cues. Learning Algorithms and Systems Laboratory, Aude Billard.

Page 31 — This ultra-high vacuum chamber, photographed open, is used to grow and characterize magnetic nanostructures. The sample is placed in the center of the line of sight, and the four conic poles of a quadrupole magnet create a magnetic field at that location. The system was custom designed by PhD students and built with help from the IPHYS mechanical workshop. Laboratory of Nanostructures at Surfaces, Harald Brune.

Page 32 — A visual representation of the virtual, this 2-bit 512-resolution matrix illustrates the final step in a major cryptanalytic computation. Laboratory for Cryptologic Algorithms, Arjen K. Lenstra.

Page 33 — The TWIICE One exoskeleton helps people with paraplegia stand, walk and even climb stairs. Weighing just 16 kg, the exoskeleton becomes one with the user, who can put it on without assistance. Robotic Systems Laboratory, Mohamed Bouri.

Page 34 — Professor Oates established a state-of-the-art automated facility on campus to enable research on birth defects, cancer, and neurological disorders. Oateslab, Andy Oates.

Page 35 — In this laboratory, chemical reactions create molecules and materials that are used to convert CO_2 into chemical products with added value. Laboratory of Nanochemistry for Energy, Raffaella Buonsanti.

Page 36 — 3D imaging by X-ray micro-tomography of a concrete sample that fractured during a compression test. The voids detected within this sample (in blue) represent either the initial bubble-shaped porosity of the concrete or the plane-shaped open fractures caused by the test. PIXE Platform, Gary Perrenoud and Pascal Turberg.

Page 37 — This in vivo mouse embryo was used to gain insight into embryo-development mechanisms in mammals and the reasons for certain malformations. Laboratory of Developmental Genomics, Denis Duboule.

Page 38 — Scanning electron micrography of cerium- and cobalt-coated steel, which is used to make fuel cells, after eight hours of oxidation at 1,100°C. Enlarged 8,000 times. Interdisciplinary Center for Electron Microscopy and the Electron Spectrometry and Microscopy Laboratory, Cécile Hébert.

Page 39 — Mechanical clock with an oscillator containing an isotropic spring called "IsoSpring" that turns continuously and could replace conventional pendulums and balance wheels. Instant-Lab, Simon Henein.

Page 40 — The acoustics in this reverberation chamber are similar to those of a cathedral. The chamber is used to study acoustic phenomena and increase understanding of how sound is created and spreads so that it can be manipulated. Signal Processing Laboratory 2, Hervé Lissek, head of the Acoustic Group.

Page 41 — The Venice Time Machine is a multidimensional model of the city spanning the past millennium, made from millions of historical documents. The Garzoni Project studies apprenticeship, work and society in early modern Venice by exploiting a specific archival source, the Accordi dei Garzoni. Digital Humanities Laboratory, Frédéric Kaplan.

Page 42 — A Drosophila larva secretes a fluorescent green protein into its blood cells, making it possible to track the movements of blood cells in vivo using a binocular magnifier. Lemaitre Lab, Bruno Lemaitre.

Page 43 — Artificial sensory skin for measuring finger movement. The skin and the electrical circuits it contains are made from highly flexible materials that move with the body. Laboratory for Soft Bioelectronic Interfaces, Stéphanie Lacour.

Page 44 — A winding machine for scintillating fiber. The fiber is wound around a one-meter-diameter wheel in six consecutive layers. In total, some 10,000 km of fiber were used to build the new tracking system in the LHCb detector, which will begin working when CERN's Large Hadron Collider restarts in 2021. Laboratory for High Energy Physics, Olivier Schneider.

Page 45 — "The Disc" in the Agora amphitheater, funded by the Fondation Lombard Odier, serves as both a cover and a tiered seating structure. Measuring 30 m in diameter and towering 6.5 meters high, it dominates the Place Cosandey. This leisure area was designed by EPFL students, under the supervision of the Design Studio on the Conception of Space, run by Dieter Dietz.

ARCHITECTURE

Bogdan Konopka

Bogdan Konopka was born in Wroclaw, Poland, in 1953 and now lives and works in Paris. After training as a photochemist, he worked in applied photography at the Wroclaw University of Science and Technology, from which he resigned under pressure from the country's political regime. He then joined the *Fotografia Elementaria* movement, but subsequently left in order to set up his own gallery, Post Scriptum. He became part of the underground artists movement and photographed his hometown with its apocalyptic atmosphere. Bogdan moved to France in 1989 and continued to capture other cities in Europe and then China, seeking to show the universal nature of the ever-changing façade of urban environments. He has been commissioned by numerous institutions to portray contemporary buildings and architecture. To ensure complete command of each step of the creative process, he uses a large-format view camera and produces contact prints. He is represented in Europe by the Françoise Paviot Gallery, Paris, and in Asia by the OFOTO Gallery, Shanghai. His work is featured in a number of large public collections, including those of the Fonds National d'Art Contemporain, the Centre Pompidou, the Bibliothèque Nationale de France, the Frac Ile-de-France and the Musée de l'Elysée in Lausanne.

BOGDAN KONOPKA

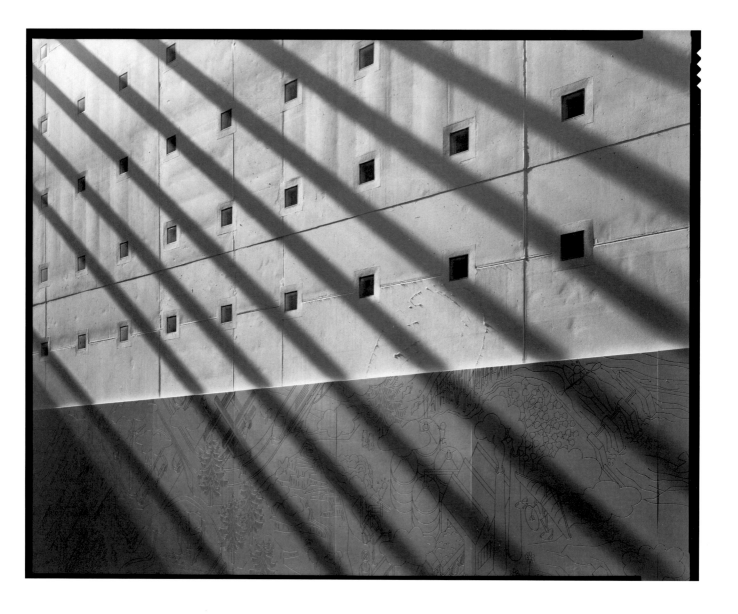

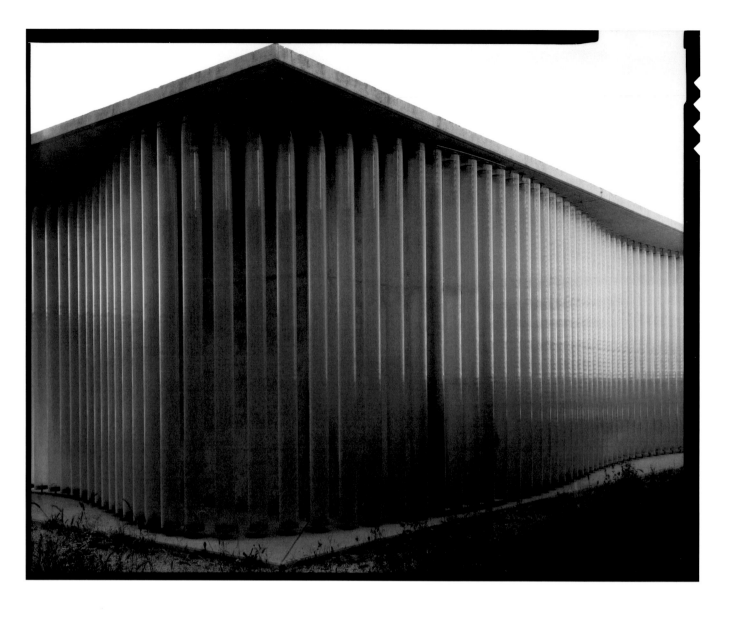

Bogdan Konopka — Architecture

Photo captions

Page 49 — Science shapes light to create a work of art under the vault of the Rolex Learning Center. When sunlight hits the large metal plates, the resulting caustic effects prompt portraits to appear. Computer Graphics and Geometry Laboratory (LGG), Marc Pauly.

Page 50 — Reflection(s), Rolex Learning Center. This building, designed by Kazuyo Sejima and Ryue Nishizawa from architecture firm SANAA, was opened in 2010 and houses, among other things, the school library and two restaurants.

Page 51 — The workshop where students from the School of Architecture, Civil and Environmental Engineering (ENAC) create their models.

Page 52 — Main auditorium, Materials Science and Engineering.

Page 53 — MX-F1 auditorium, Materials Science and Engineering.

Page 54 — Wall enclosing the Variable Configuration Tokamak, the fusion reactor in the Swiss Plasma Center.

Page 55 — Close-up of the Variable Configuration Tokamak, the fusion reactor in the Swiss Plasma Center.

Page 56 — Archizoom. This on-campus architecture museum hosts the exhibitions and conferences organized by the School of Architecture, Civil and Environmental Engineering (ENAC).

Page 57 — Sitting area in the Swiss-Tech Convention Center, EPFL Quartier Nord.

Page 58 — Solar panels on the roof of the Microcity building, EPFL Neuchâtel.

Page 59 — EPFL Valais-Wallis, Sion. This outpost is devoted primarily to scientific research in energy, health and the environment.

Page 60 — Center of MicroNanoTechnology, Microengineering building. The building is linked to the BP and SG buildings. Designed by Zurich-based architects Schnebli Ammann Menz and Flora Ruchat-Roncati.

Page 61 — A look inside the Center of MicroNanoTechnology, Micro-engineering building.

Page 62 — The new Mechanical Engineering building, designed by Dominique Perrault, reflected in the ArtLab building, designed by Kengo Kuma.

Page 63 — Inside the new Mechanical Engineering building.

Pages 64-65 — Rolex Learning Center. The large interior landscape was designed to be very accessible to the public. In the background, to the left, is the Odyssea building, which used to belong to Swisscom and now houses the College of Management of Technology. It was designed by architect Rodolph Luscher and was one of the first buildings in Switzerland with a double-skin facade to control airflow and sunlight.

Page 66 — Large leisure area in front of the Giacometti cafeteria, between the BP, BM and SG buildings.

Page 67 — The GA building, which is home to Polychinelle, a nursery for children over the age of three months; Polykids, which covers the first two years of primary school; and the Science Outreach Department, which organizes workshops and other extracurricular activities for children, as well as events for schools and the general public.

Page 68 — View, from the Esplanade, of the new Mechanical Engineering building, the Rolex Learning Center and the ArtLab building.

Page 69 — The campus reflected in the Rolex Learning Center.

Page 70 — View from outside the Copernic restaurant.

Page 71 — EPFL Fribourg. Since 2015, EPFL Fribourg has been housed at the Smart Living Lab, an R&D center dedicated to the built environment of the future, in the blueFACTORY innovation park.

Page 72 — The PPB building, which runs along the main road. It was built by Lausanne-based architectural firm Atelier Cube in 1987 and houses the Plasma Physics Research Center.

Page 73 — The Polydôme, designed by Julius Natterer and John MacIntyre in 1993. Julius Natterer was head of the IBOIS lab and an EPFL professor.

Page 74 — View from the top of the BC building, which houses the School of Computer and Communication Sciences.

Page 75 — View of the Alps from the top of the BC building, which houses the School of Computer and Communication Sciences.

Page 76 — Stairwell inside the BC building, designed by architect Rodolph Luscher.

Page 77 — Campus Biotech, Geneva. This building, which hosts EPFL research groups in the fields of biotechnology, neuroscience and neuroprosthetics, is located in the former industrial district of Sécheron. The building uses lake water as its primary source of energy, which considerably reduces its environmental impact.

Page 78 — The Diagonale gets its name from the story of how the campus was built. After the initial construction phase, the positioning of new campus buildings had to be carefully considered. So in the 1980s, the Diagonale was laid out and various architects were hired to design new buildings around it.

Page 79 — Light well in the Civil Engineering building.

PEOPLE

Olivier Christinat

Olivier Christinat was born on 19 December 1963 and trained as a photographer in Lausanne from 1980 to 1984. He started out as a freelance photographer in 1985. From 1996 he worked primarily on his own projects, creating three photo series — *Photographies apocryphes*, *Evènements* and *Nues*. In 2001, the 2002 Swiss National Expo commissioned him to produce the images for an exhibition entitled *Le premier regard* in Yverdon-les-Bains. Alongside his own projects, he has taught photography at the CFPArts school in Geneva since 2003. In 2004, Olivier was chosen by SRG SSR idée suisse as one of 28 photographers to be included in Photo Suisse, a large-scale project that involved a book on the artists' work, a series of documentaries and a worldwide exhibition. Olivier decided to change course in 2010, when he left his workshop and studio to create the photo series *Leçon de paysage*, *Autre leçon de paysage*, *Lignes de fuite* and *Nouveaux Souvenirs*. His talent has been recognized on numerous occasions: he was awarded the Rado Star Prize Switzerland 2013 at the Biel/Bienne Festival of Photography and was invited to take part in an exhibition entitled *Un autre regard sur Paléo* at the Musée de l'Elysée, Lausanne, in 2015. A collection of his post-2010 work has been compiled in a book, *Nouveaux souvenirs*.

OLIVIER CHRISTINAT

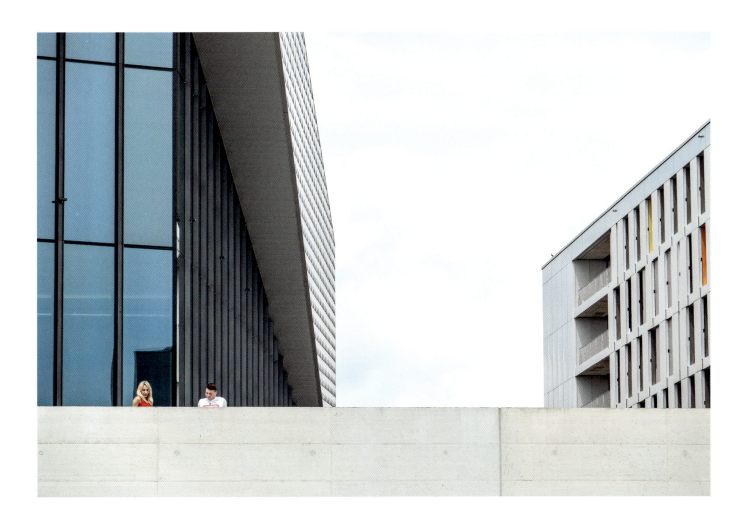

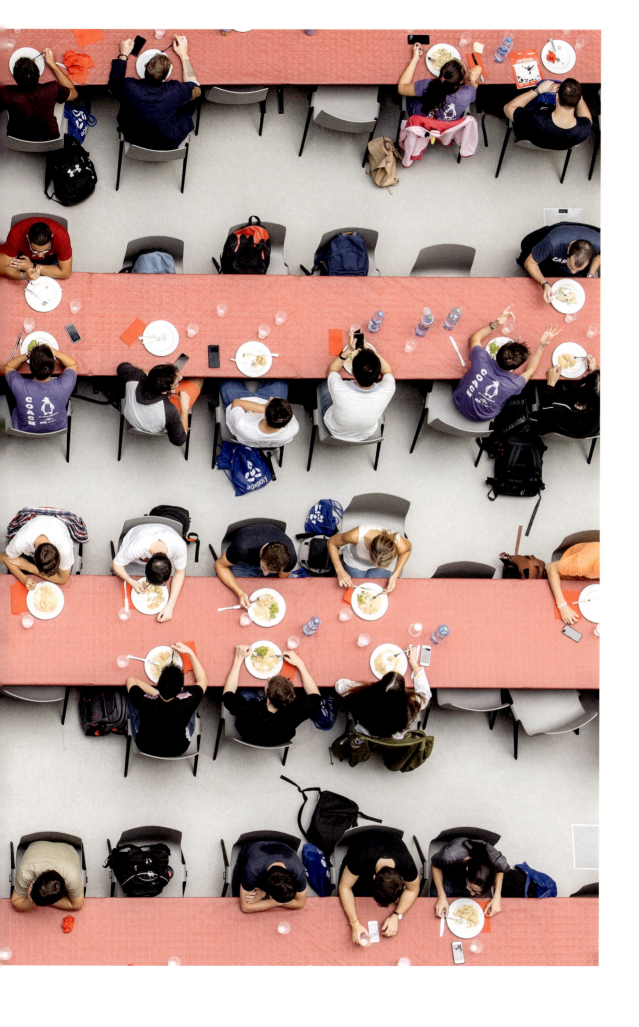

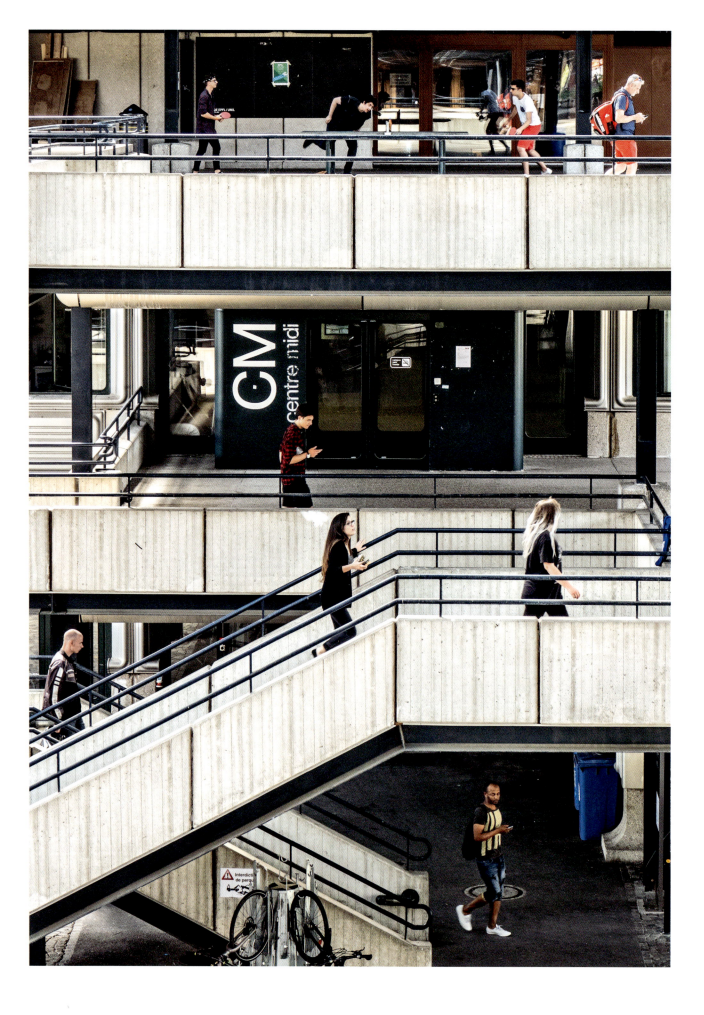

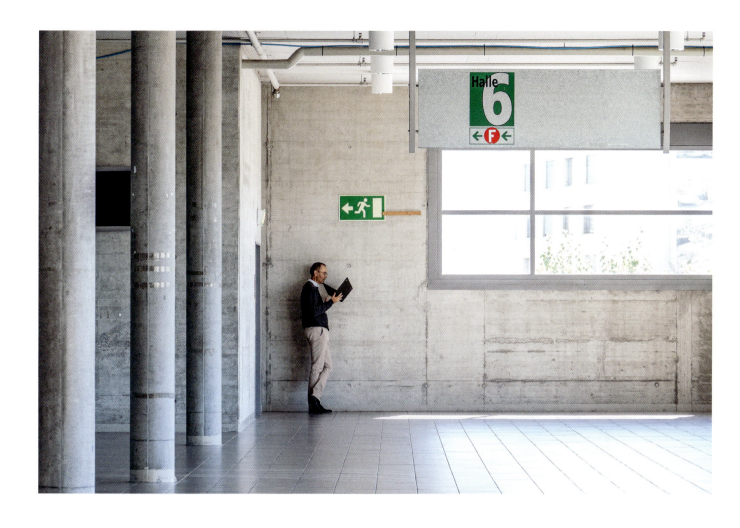

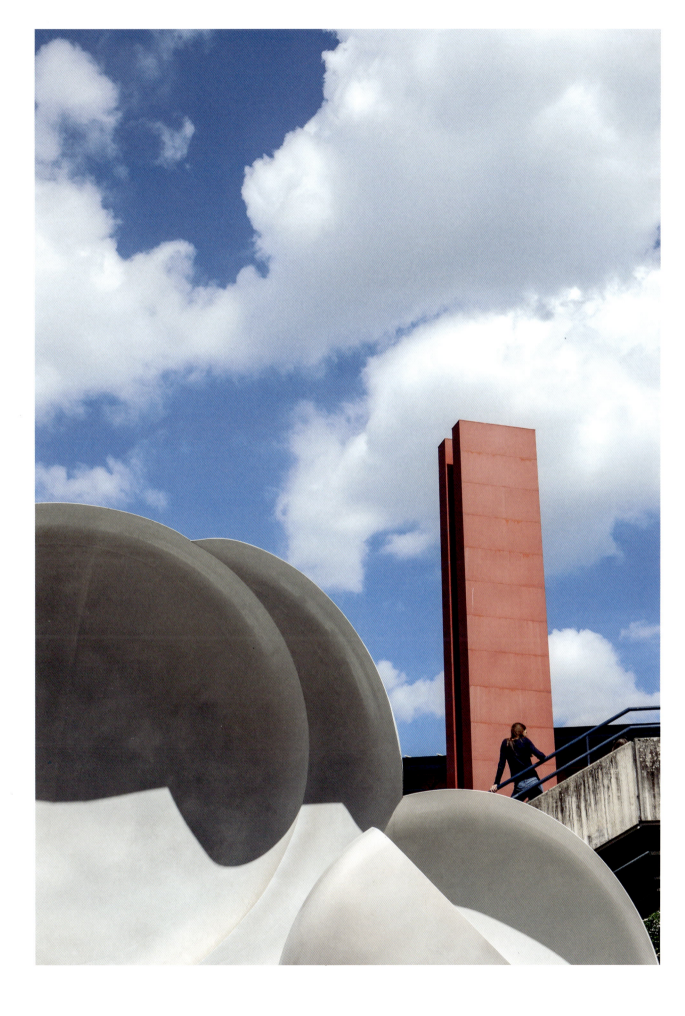

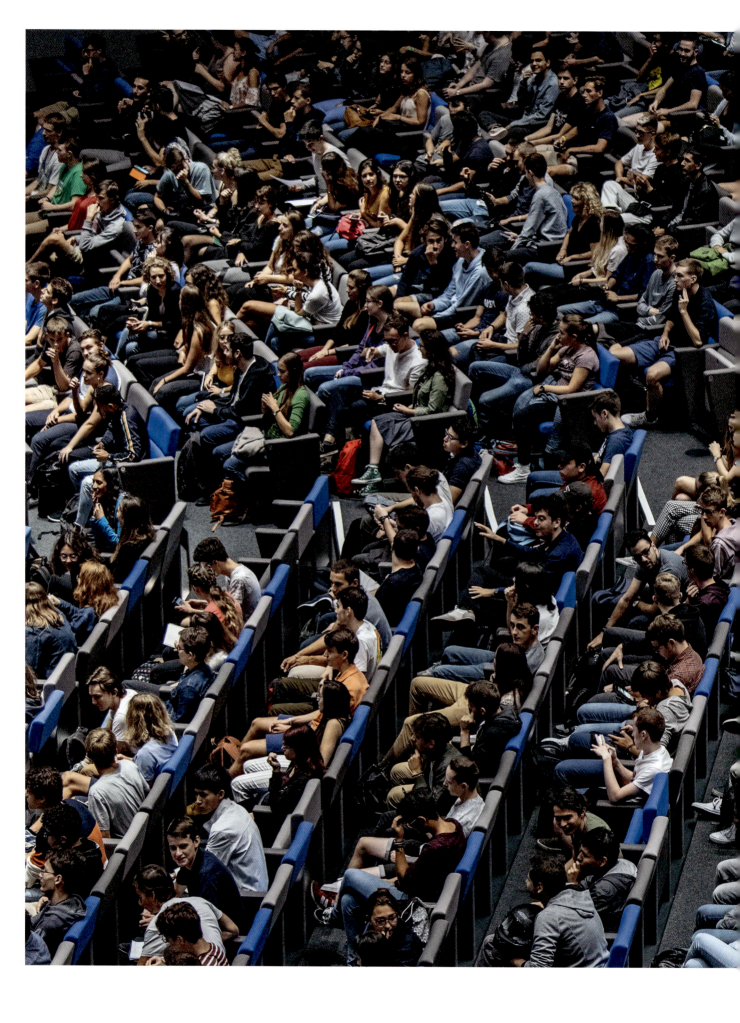

Olivier Christinat — People

Photo captions

Page 83 — Life on the Lausanne campus. Out of EPFL's 11,134 students, 3,250 are women (29%) and 7,884 are men (71%).

Pages 84-85 — Welcome Day for new students, 14 September 2018.

Page 86 — Life on the Lausanne campus. These buildings were designed by Zweifel, Strickler and Partners in Zurich. They were part of the first phase of the campus' construction, in 1977. This modular architecture is arranged orthogonally. Walkways, public areas and offices are located on the upper floor, while the lecture halls and classrooms are on the middle floor. The lower floor is for deliveries.

Page 87 — Campus Biotech, Geneva. This building houses a center of excellence in biotechnology and life science research, which was set up in 2013 by EPFL, the University of Geneva, the Bertarelli family and Hansjörg Wyss. The building uses lake water as its primary source of energy, which considerably reduces its environmental impact.

Page 88 — Students getting in their seats before the class "Materials: from chemistry to properties" taught by Eva Klok-Lermann and Véronique Michaud. The course teaches key concepts that relate the structure of matter, equilibria and chemical reactivity to the mechanical, thermal, electrical, magnetic and optical properties of materials.

Page 89 — Life on campus. Mensa eating area, Campus Biotech, Geneva.

Page 90 — Life on campus. Taken at the BC building, which houses the School of Computer and Communication Sciences.

Page 91 — Large leisure area in front of the Giacometti cafeteria, between the BP, BM and SG buildings, which host architectural and life-science students.

Page 92 — The "General physics: mechanics" class. Philippe Müllhaupt teaches students the core principles required to understand physical phenomena.

Page 93 — Students from the School of Architecture, Civil and Environmental Engineering.

Page 94 — Taking a break, Life Sciences building.

Page 95 — Science and teaching days, Fribourg. These events bring EPFL professors together to discuss important topics in teaching, research and innovation.

Page 96 — Lab work.

Page 97 — The human in the machine (1).

Pages 98-99 — Capturing the moment. Mensa eating area, School of Life Sciences.

Pages 100 and 101 — Balélec Festival 2018, 38th edition. This student-run event takes place every year in May on the EPFL campus. With some 15,000 attendees, it is one of the largest outdoor music festivals in Switzerland. It started out as a ball held by EPFL's Electrical Engineering department.

Page 102 — The human in the machine (2).

Page 103 — On the sidelines of the Magistrale, EPFL's graduation ceremony.

Page 104 — Inside the new Mechanical Engineering building.

Page 105 — Perspective(s). In front of the Microengineering building.

Page 106 — Studying for exams in the Rolex Learning Center library.

Page 107 — Art at EPFL. Seventeen sculptures by both Swiss and foreign artists are spread over campus. Foreground: "Echochrome," by Gillian White and Albert Siegenthaler, 1985.

Page 108 — Science and teaching days, Fribourg. These events bring EPFL professors together to discuss important topics in teaching, research and innovation.

Pages 109-112 — Studying for exams in the Rolex Learning Center library.

Page 113 — The 2018 Magistrale, EPFL's graduation ceremony.

Pages 114-115 — Welcome Day for new students.

EPFL IN THE
WORDS OF
ITS PRESIDENTS

Maurice Cosandey
Jean-Claude Badoux
Patrick Aebischer
Martin Vetterli

Martin Vetterli, Jean-Claude Badoux, Patrick Aebischer and Maurice Cosandey.
18 May 2018 © Olivier Christinat

When I became president of the Ecole polytechnique de l'Université de Lausanne (EPUL), I dreamed of transforming the School into a federal institute of technology. So I quickly got down to work with the freshly elected Vaud State Councillor, Jean-Pierre Pradervand, who headed the Vaud Canton Department of Education. We went to Bern to meet with Federal Councillor Hans-Peter Tschudi at the Schweizerhof restaurant. At the end of the meal, Mr. Tschudi suggested that the Vaud Cantonal Government submit a request to the Federal Council. So we got the ball rolling as soon as we returned to Lausanne.

Just before the Swiss parliament voted unanimously in favor of turning the School into a federal institute, I was talking to Hans-Peter Tschudi about the future, and he said: "You know, if your School wasn't so good, we wouldn't have accepted it." That was a real tribute to my predecessor, Professor Alfred Stucky, who ran the School for 23 years and brought EPUL, which had previously been scattered across Lausanne, under one roof on the magnificent Cèdres site in Ouchy (the old Hôtel Savoy).

Once the School became a federal institute of technology, the first thing I did was to submit a loan application for the construction of a sports hall on the site owned jointly by the University of Lausanne and EPFL. I wrote to the federal government seeking half the required funding. I was summoned to Bern to discuss the matter with two members of the committee in charge of submitting the proposal to Parliament. At first, they were surprised that they had been asked for money to build a sports hall, but I soon brought them around.

Having reached the ripe old age of one hundred, I would like to thank everyone who has helped me throughout my career. I am very happy to see how the School is developing, and I wish EPFL all the best for the future. But in today's world, it pains me to see how humans can act so irresponsibly and selfishly. I wish that all the children in the world could be fed and raised like my great grandchildren, Quentin, Simon, Félicien, Ferdinand, Jeanne, Eva-Rose and Astrid. But for that, we need peace. And to achieve peace we need to eliminate weapons and the distrust they create — and we also need hope. As the philosopher Pierre Teilhard de Chardin said: may we combine and strengthen our individual intelligence in order to build humanity's collective conscience.

EPFL CREATED BY A UNANIMOUS VOTE

Maurice Cosandey
(08.02.1918 - 04.12.2018)
EPFL president from 1963 to 1978

When I became president, in December 1992, Bernard Vittoz's management team helped me prepare for the twists and turns on the road ahead. I had a feeling that the budget would be tight over the coming years, but I was very firm about what the School's priorities and "posteriorities" were — and that was new for EPFL. The focus was on microengineering and communication systems, along with bioengineering, all areas that expanded considerably over the subsequent eight years. At the same time, I initiated a major reorganization of the subjects taught at EPFL, the University of Lausanne and the University of Geneva. As a result, in 1999, EPFL added chemistry, physics and mathematics to its existing courses on chemical engineering, physical engineering and applied mathematics. This allowed the School to obtain a budget increase of 10%, representing an extra 50 million Swiss francs a year.

I also wanted to strengthen the teaching staff. A number of new positions for professors and lecturers were created, and more value was placed on experience acquired outside of academia. We also introduced major incentives to increase the number of doctoral students. In addition, I built ties with other academic institutions around the world, and I opened EPFL up to Russia and Asia, especially India and South Korea. We also strengthened our collaboration with ETH Zurich — although I liked to call it EPFZ. For me, it seemed only right that EPFL's strongest partner should be in the German-speaking part of the country.

Another of my priorities was to increase the proportion of women at EPFL. The number of female professors rose tenfold under my leadership, and I introduced various measures aimed at helping women kick start their academic careers. I also worked the political levers in order to ensure the School had the funding needed for its expansion. These efforts paid off: we had 150 professors in 1992 and over 250 by 2000.

Appointing professors took up about 40% of my time. It requires real intuition and commitment. Back in the spring of 1966, Maurice Cosandey brought me over from California for an interview, and he alone made the decision to hire me as a professor at EPUL. In the summer of 1992, before taking up office as president, I invited a promising young professor from Columbia University to my home. I made the decision to hire him and signed the contract that same day. The man in question was Professor Martin Vetterli, the School's current president.

BRANCHING OUT INTO NEW FIELDS

Jean-Claude Badoux
EPFL president from 1992 to 2000

In the 1960s, Federal Councillor Hans-Peter Tschudi, Vaud State Councillor Jean-Pierre Pradervand and the School's then-President Maurice Cosandey changed the course of history for EPUL, which at the time was a respected regional university. It is thanks to the unfailing commitment and perseverance of these three visionaries that EPUL was turned into a Swiss federal institute of technology on 1 January 1969, paving the way for EPFL to become the internationally renowned institute of science and technology it is today.

The skyline of our School's hometown, Ecublens, is never short of construction cranes as EPFL seeks to create an appealing, state-of-the-art campus equipped with all the requisite classrooms, high-end laboratories, places to eat and relax, and student accommodations — not to mention the sports facilities the School shares with its neighbor, the University of Lausanne. The famous Rolex Learning Center is just one of the truly pioneering buildings found on campus. And to ensure that the rest of French-speaking Switzerland can reap the benefits of having a world-renowned school at its doorstep, EPFL has also set up campuses in Neuchâtel, Sion, Geneva and Fribourg. The School has set its sights high, and its global ambitions are paying off — the number of students from all over the world attending EPFL has risen steadily and stands at more than 10,000 today, and EPFL attracts some of the best researchers and professors from around the globe. What's more, flagship projects like Alinghi, Solar Impulse, the Human Brain Project and the Venice Time Machine have helped cultivate the School's spirit and enhance the School's visibility. Over the years, members of the EPFL community have put their skills and determination to work to find solutions to the greatest challenges we face today, from mobility and global warming to the use of biotechnology and artificial intelligence. The quality of the teaching and research at EPFL is reflected in the School's international rankings. The campus has also become a breeding ground for tech startups that play a key role in the local economy.

But this success should not be taken for granted. Global competition is fierce, and the risk of bureaucratic overreach is ever-present. EPFL would not be where it is today without strong leadership and staff who truly identify with their School — or without the generous support it receives from both the Swiss federal government and the region's cantonal governments. I hope that EPFL will continue to live the dream for the next 50 years too. That is my greatest wish, for the good of our region and Switzerland as a whole.

LONG LIVE EPFL!

Patrick Aebischer
EPFL president from 2000 to 2016

It's like something out of a poem: a campus located just a stone's throw from the shores of Lake Geneva with the Alps as its backdrop. The architecture, like the School itself, is ambitious in design, with a number of groundbreaking and iconic buildings. And the campus community — some 15,000 students, staff and professors — brings it all to life.

EPFL is just 50 years old, which makes it a youngster in the cohort of research universities around the world — but that also means it's still very much in its prime.

As it comes of age, EPFL has done its soul-searching and found its place: it's an entrepreneurial school that strives to have a positive impact on society; and it's looking ahead yet ready and willing to seize any opportunities that arise along the way. After all, EPFL has already gone through a number of changes. It parted ways with the University of Lausanne and left its old name, Ecole polytechnique de l'Université de Lausanne (EPUL), behind. It has transformed from an engineering school into a research university. And it has expanded its repertoire in physical and life sciences, engineering and architecture.

Very early on, technology transfer became a key mission for EPFL, which created an innovation park long before that became the trend in Switzerland. This desire to contribute to society is a source of inspiration for researchers and allows the knowledge acquired in the School's laboratories to be shared. It is this synergy that drives the innovation ecosystem both in the region and throughout Switzerland. Alongside education and research, tech transfer is one of EPFL's three core missions — and one it has fulfilled with great success. But research will always be the backbone of the campus, which is home to some 350 faculty-run laboratories. Professors are knowledge entrepreneurs, plotting a course through uncharted territory and preparing the next generation of scientists for a unique adventure in cutting-edge research.

Finally, there can be no research and innovation without education and training, a fundamental and eminently noble mission. Imparting knowledge, explaining new ideas and laying strong foundations — these are the essential ingredients of an education for life.

As it turns 50, EPFL is looking to the future. The 21st century will be filled with worthy challenges for an institute of technology. From fundamental research to technological progress and social betterment, there's no shortage of crucial questions: How can we make development sustainable for our planet? What are the limits of artificial intelligence? How can we control genetic engineering? What can we do to better understand the brain and interface with it? And the list goes on. At the same time, we must not forget our responsibility towards society — it is our role to train scientists, engineers and architects who will help make the world a better place. I'm sure that in 2069, when EPFL marks its 100th anniversary, it will be proud of what it has achieved for humanity.

Until then, this book takes a look back at what EPFL accomplished in its first 50 years.

EPFL — YOUNG AND PROUD

Martin Vetterli
EPFL president starting in 2017

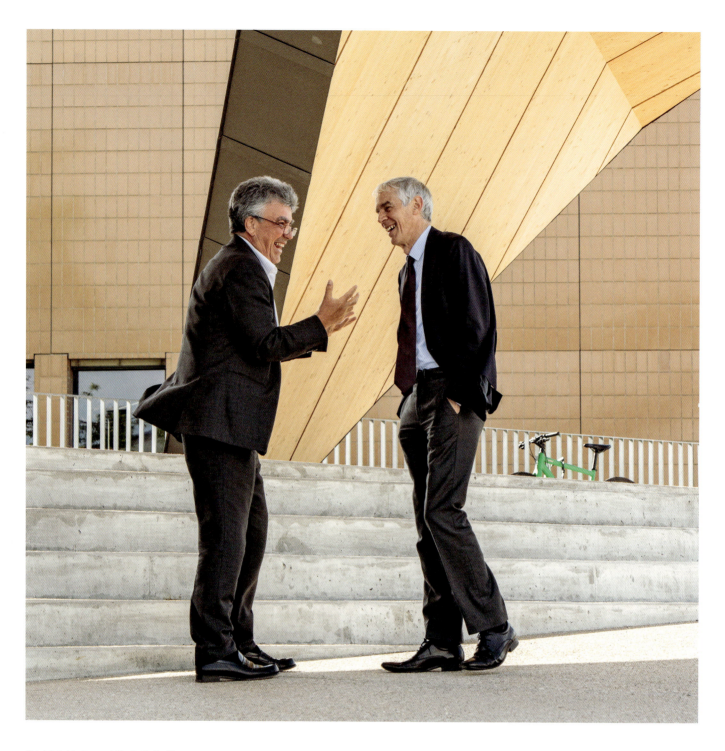

Patrick Aebischer and Martin Vetterli.
© Olivier Christinat

1853 — The Ecole spéciale de Lausanne is founded on a private initiative. It has 11 students.

1944 — The School moves to the old Hôtel Savoy on the Avenue de Cour in Lausanne.

1946 — The School's name is changed to Ecole polytechnique de l'Université de Lausanne, or EPUL.

1953 — EPUL marks its centenary year. It has 45 professors and lecturers and 508 students.

1963 — Maurice Cosandey, the future founder of EPFL, becomes president of EPUL. The School has 1,087 students.

1969 — EPFL officially becomes a federal institute of technology on 1 January, with Maurice Cosandey selecting the School's departments and research fields.

1977 — EPFL moves out of Lausanne to its current campus.

1978 — Bernard Vittoz succeeds Maurice Cosandey as president. He strengthens ties between EPFL and the business world and creates the Science Park, which plays host to a number of EPFL spin-offs. He also adds further research fields, such as mathematics, materials science and microengineering. The School has 1,750 students.

1992 — Jean-Claude Badoux, EPFL's third president, realigns the School's priorities, with a focus on microengineering, communication systems, management and economics. The School has 3,912 students.

2000 — Patrick Aebischer leads the School's reorganization into five faculties, creates the Faculty of Life Sciences and expands EPFL across French-speaking Switzerland. He also commissions the construction of a number of iconic buildings on campus, including the Rolex Learning Center. The School has 4,899 students.

2009 — Microcity, a microengineering and nanotechnology hub, is created in Neuchâtel.

2014 —EPFL Valais Wallis, specializing in industrial energy, green chemistry, environmental engineering, biotechnology and bioengineering, is opened, as is EPFL Fribourg, which is centered on building technology and sustainable architecture.

2015 — The Geneva Biotech Campus, home to the Wyss Center, the Human Brain Project and the Center of Neuroprosthetics, is founded.

2017 — Martin Vetterli becomes president, positioning EPFL at the forefront of the response to the challenges of digitalization and open science in Switzerland. The School has 10,686 students.

EPFL — A BRIEF HISTORY

EPFL wishes to thank the three photographers — Catherine Leutenegger, Bogdan Konopka and Olivier Christinat — whose talent and generosity went into the creation of this book.

We are also grateful to Tatyana Franck, the director of the Musée de l'Elysée photography museum in Lausanne. As the president of the editorial committee, whose task was to select the photographers and photographs, she provided valuable expertise throughout the creative and publishing process. Our thanks naturally go to the other members of the editorial committee as well.

Finally, we would like to express our gratitude to Alain Herzog, Christine Metzler, Cyril Veillon, the researchers and everyone else who facilitated the photographers' work or who contributed in some way to the creation of this book and the ArtLab exhibition.

ACKNOWLEDGMENTS

Published by EPFL to mark its 50th anniversary as a federal institute of technology. Created in collaboration with the Musée de l'Elysée, in Lausanne.

Editorial committee (photo selection):
Tatyana Franck, president
Sarah Kenderdine
Tristan Maillard
Sabine Süsstrunk
Martin Vetterli
Editorial coordinator:
Corinne Feuz
Graphic designer:
Valérie Giroud
Photo editor:
Roger Emmenegger
Printer:
Genoud Arts graphiques SA
English translations:
Scala Wells Sàrl
Communications:
Mediacom, EPFL

www.epfl.ch

First edition
ISBN 978-2-88915-305-3

EPFL Press is the English-language imprint of Presses polytechniques et universitaires romandes.
EPFL, Rolex Learning Center, CP 119
CH – 1015 Lausanne
www.ppur.org
The texts and photographs are copyrighted by their respective creators.
©EPFL, PPUR 2019 / All rights reserved. The reproduction of all or part of this publication, on any medium whatsoever, is strictly forbidden without the publisher's prior written authorization.

IMPRESSUM